HARRY HOUDINI

HARRY HOUDINI

Master Magician
by Dana Meachen Rau

A Book Report Biography
FRANKLIN WATTS
A Division of Grolier Publishing
New York / London / Hong Kong / Sydney
Danbury, Connecticut

Cover illustration by Dave Klaboe,
interpreted from a photograph ©: Corbis-Bettmann/UPI.

Frontispiece: Harry Houdini before performing his underwater
handcuff escape in Boston, Massachusetts, 1906

Photographs ©: Brown Brothers: 69, 79; Corbis-Bettmann: 71 (Under-
wood & Underwood), chapter openers, 85, 93, 95 (UPI), 2, 20, 43, 59, 64;
Houdini Historical Center, Appleton, Wisconsin: 14 (Boldt Collection), 56
(Hyman Collection); Houdini Historical Center, Appleton, Wisconsin/
Sidney H. Radner Collection: 10, 25, 53, 61, 66, 77; Kevin A. Connolly: 16,
23, 31, 82; Library of Congress: 29, 41.

Visit Franklin Watts on the Internet at:
http://publishing.grolier.com

Library of Congress Cataloging-in-Publication Data

Rau, Dana Meachen, 1971–
    Harry Houdini, master magician / by Dana Meachen Rau.
        p. cm.—(Book report biography)
    Includes bibliographical references and index.
    ISBN 0-531-11599-2 (lib. bdg.)   0-531-15551-X (pbk.)
    1. Houdini, Harry, 1874–1926—Juvenile literature. 2. Magicians—
United States—Biography—Juvenile literature. 3. Escape artists—United
States—Biography—Juvenile literature. [1. Houdini, Harry, 1874–1926. 2.
Magicians.] I. Title. II. Series.

    GV1545.H8 R38 2001
    793.8'092—dc21
    [B]   00-039930

CONTENTS

HARRY HOUDINI

CHAPTER ONE

THE ESCAPE ARTIST

At noon on November 6, 1916, Houdini arrived at the tall office building of the *Sun*, a city newspaper in Pittsburgh, Pennsylvania. The feat he was about to perform guaranteed Houdini a front-page article in the next day's newspaper. A crowd of 20,000 people crammed into Wood Street and Liberty Avenue.

Houdini took a straitjacket out of his bag. It was the kind of straitjacket used to restrain the criminally insane. A committee confirmed that the straitjacket had not been tampered with. Then two men strapped Houdini in. "Make it tight," he said.

They fastened Houdini's ankles to a rope. A system of pulleys attached to the office building lifted him higher and higher. Soon he dangled more than five stories above the hard pavement.

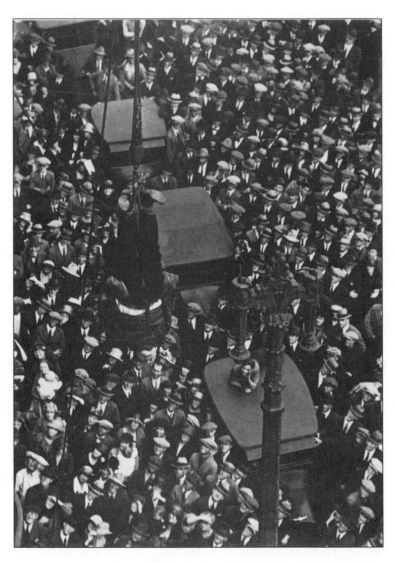

Harry Houdini hangs suspended in a straitjacket above a crowded street in Pittsburgh.

As the newspaper reported the next day:

While watchers gleamed in the crowd below, the handcuff king was seen to struggle, not frantically, but with a steady, systematic swelling and contracting of muscles. . . . The struggle went on. One minute—two—then three—Would he do it?

Amazingly, Houdini's wiggling and writhing had freed his body from the straitjacket. He flung it to the ground. The newspaper declared, "Houdini had triumphed—as he always triumphs."

The suspended straitjacket escape in Pittsburgh was just one of many amazing feats Houdini performed throughout the United States. Crowds gathered everywhere to catch a glimpse of him. He was the most recognized magician in the world.

That escape was a sight most people would never forget. Like all Houdini's stunts, the danger was very real. At any moment, he could fall to certain death. Houdini wanted his stunts to be as impressive as possible and for as big an audience as could fit in the streets below. He loved the publicity. In fact, to get the most press, he usually did the stunt hanging from the building of each city's newspaper.

Houdini's career was a mixture of tricks, illusions, and death-defying stunts. And his ability to wow his audiences was due to his well-developed athletic skill, keen wit and intelligence, and nimble fingers and toes to pick locks. He knew how to get attention.

Even though he was not a tall man—Houdini stood 5 feet 6 inches (168 cm) tall—he was definitely larger than life. Always a man who voiced his opinion, he had one about his stature as well: "The best men are not too high. . . . All the keen, eager, ambitious men—short!"

CHAPTER TWO

THE MAGICIAN FINDS HIS WAY

Harry Houdini was a mysterious character. He was even secretive about where he was born. Perhaps to appeal to American audiences, Houdini claimed he was born in Appleton, Wisconsin. But records show that he didn't arrive in Appleton until he was four years old.

Harry Houdini's real name was Ehrich Weiss. He was born on March 24, 1874, in Budapest, Hungary, to Samuel and Cecilia Weiss. Samuel Weiss was a rabbi—a Jewish religious leader. In 1876, Samuel decided to leave for the United States. He had heard of opportunities there and wanted to get away from Budapest's anti-Semitism—discrimination against Jewish people.

Two years later, Samuel Weiss found himself in Appleton, Wisconsin. He started a small Jewish synagogue and served as rabbi. Now settled, he sent for his family. Cecilia packed up four-year-old

*Harry Houdini's father, Samuel Weiss,
was a rabbi.*

Ehrich, her other three young sons, and Herman, Samuel's fourteen-year-old son from his first marriage. They boarded a ship named the *Frisia* and traveled fifteen days in steerage class, a part of the boat reserved for the poorest passengers. The *Frisia* arrived in New York City on July 3, 1878, and the family soon joined Samuel Weiss in Appleton.

Appleton was a small American town, and Samuel Weiss and his family did not fit in as well as he had hoped. He led his religious services in German. The congregation may have wanted a more modern American leader. After less than four years, the synagogue let Samuel Weiss go.

Samuel then moved his family to the larger city of Milwaukee, Wisconsin. Although Milwaukee had a large Jewish population, it had only two synagogues. Samuel couldn't find a job to support his wife and growing family, which now had seven children—Herman, Nathan, William, Ehrich, Theodore, Leopold, and Carrie Gladys.

Samuel took temporary jobs and moved his family around Milwaukee. He ran a private school for a time, but his family still had to struggle to get by. Ehrich helped out by shining shoes, selling newspapers, and doing odd jobs around the neighborhood.

When Ehrich was twelve, he ran away from home to try to make money for the family else-

Harry Houdini at age eight

where. He wanted to head to Texas, but he jumped onto the wrong train car and ended up in Missouri. Then he went to Delavan, Wisconsin, just 50 miles (80 km) from Milwaukee. Believing he was homeless, a couple took him in while he worked as a shoeshine boy.

A MOVE TO NEW YORK CITY

Like Ehrich, Samuel Weiss was feeling the strain of poverty. He decided to try New York City, which had a much larger Jewish population. He and Ehrich went there together in 1887. Cecilia and the other children joined them the next year.

"We lived there—I mean starved there, several years," Houdini said. Samuel Weiss did religious work when he could, but without any real success. Ehrich tried to supplement the family income by working as a messenger boy. According to one family story, the family was so poor one winter that Ehrich had to beg for coins. After an unusually successful day, he hid the coins in his clothes. When he arrived home that evening, he told his mother, "Shake me! I'm magic!" As she shook him, the coins showered on a very grateful family.

Because he was always working, Ehrich never had much time for school, although he did get some education from a local Jewish school. In

1888, he found a more regular job with a tie manufacturer called H. Richter's Sons.

In the little free time he had, Ehrich excelled in sports. He loved to swim and box, and he ran up to 10 miles (16 km) a day. He joined the Amateur Athletic Union and the Pastime Athletic Club and competed in their races. This stimulated his deeply competitive nature —a trait that would always define Houdini's character. "I want to be first," he once said. "I vehemently want to be first. First in my profession, in my specialty in my profession. For that I give all the thought, all the power that is in me."

"I want to be first. I vehemently want to be first. First in my profession, in my specialty in my profession."

When Ehrich Weiss was seventeen, his trademark body—strong, stocky, and athletic—was already clear. His thick neck, muscular body, and slightly bowed legs displayed the strength that would be so important in the challenges to come.

THE BEGINNINGS OF MAGIC

It is difficult to trace exactly when Ehrich's interest in magic began. Years later, as a successful magician, Houdini often published pamphlets that exaggerated stories from his youth to promote his act. As a result, it's hard to tell which tales are true.

Houdini often said he was hypnotized watching magicians perform and was fascinated with life in the circus when he was young. When he was nine, he convinced a circus to pay him thirty-five cents to pick up needles with his eyelashes while hanging upside down. He also performed a trapeze act wearing red stockings and calling himself Ehrich, Prince of the Air.

Some of Ehrich's best friends as a teenager were also interested in magic—Joe Rinn was a fellow athlete from the Pastime Athletic Club, and Jacob Hyman was a friend from Richter's tie factory. Soon, Ehrich and Jacob (who changed his name to Jack Hayman to sound more American) performed a magic act at private parties.

Ehrich's interest in magic grew. He first read the life story, or memoirs, of Jean Eugène Robert-Houdin in 1889. Robert-Houdin (1805–1871) was a famous French magician, often called the founder of modern magic. His memoirs tell of a young man, alone in the world, who works his way up to becoming a great magician. Houdini may have identified with him, since he too was looking for a direction in life. "My interest in conjuring and magic and my enthusiasm for Robert-Houdin came into existence simultaneously. From the

Jean Eugène Robert-Houdin, the founder of modern magic, was a role model for young Ehrich.

moment that I began to study the art, he became my guide and hero," Houdini once said.

When Ehrich decided he wanted a career in magic, he changed his name, which was a common practice among magicians. He added an "i" to "Houdin," which in French means "like Houdin." He also changed his first name to Harry, an Americanization of his nickname, Ehrie.

THE BROTHERS HOUDINI

In 1891, Harry and Jack took their show on the road and called themselves the Brothers Houdini. They found work in dime museums (small museums where audiences paid a dime to see ten acts), small theaters in New York and the Midwest, amusement parks, and beer halls.

After saving up some money, Houdini bought his first illusion—a magic trick and the equipment needed to do it. Many magicians bought and sold illusions. Newspapers or magazines listed advertisements selling these tricks and the equipment needed for them. The first illusion Houdini purchased was a trunk trick called Metamorphosis. It was one of his most popular illusions for the rest of his life.

Eventually, Jack left the Brothers Houdini. Houdini replaced Jack with his real brother, Theodore, who used the nickname Dash (for his dashing good looks). Harry and Dash were partners, but Dash knew Harry was "very decidedly the boss."

Dubbing themselves the Modern Monarchs of Mystery, the Brothers Houdini performed at the 1893 World's Columbian Exposition in Chicago. (Here, visitors also tasted Aunt Jemima pancake mix and rode a Ferris wheel for the first time.) As a sideshow, the Brothers Houdini earned twelve dollars a week for twenty shows a day. They entertained audiences with rope, card, and handkerchief tricks, and their trademark Metamorphosis. Also in 1893, Houdini did a handcuff act for the first time, calling himself "Harry Houdini, Handcuff King and Escape Artist."

The Brothers Houdini were a success, and Harry and Dash sent the extra money they earned home to help their mother. (When their father died of cancer in 1892, Harry had promised him that he would always take care of his mother.) But in the summer of 1894, the brothers' partnership ended. Harry had found a new partner in life and in magic—his wife.

A NEW PARTNER

Houdini's marriage was so sudden that some have said it was as if Houdini turned twenty, decided it was about time to get married, and immediately

*Harry (standing) and his brother Dash performed as
the Brothers Houdini at the 1893 World's Columbian
Exposition in Chicago, Illinois.*

went out and did just that. We know Harry first met Wilhelmina Beatrice Rahner (known as Bess) in 1894, but how they met depends on who you ask.

In a magazine interview, Houdini explained: "One day I was hired to give an exhibition at a children's party in Brooklyn. At the close a little girl, about sixteen, said to me very bashfully, 'I think you are awfully clever,' and then, with a blush, 'I like you.' 'How much do you like me?' I said, 'enough to marry me?' We had never seen each other before. She nodded. And so, after talking the matter over, we were married."

Bess gives a different account. In her 1928 biography of her husband, written after his death, she describes their first meeting. Harry Houdini had come to her high school to perform, and Bess and her mother sat in the front row. During the show, Harry spilled some acid on her dress and ruined it. Harry brought a new dress that his mother had made to Bess's house, and she was thrilled. They took off for Coney Island, but Bess was worried about what her mother would think. Harry said, "If you were my wife they wouldn't dare punish you." So they tried on rings and got married.

The most likely story is that his brother Dash first met Bess when she was performing in a song-and-dance act called the Floral Sisters. Dash

Harry Houdini and Bess Rahner were married
soon after they met.

arranged for Bess and Harry to meet, and it was love at first sight. After only a few weeks, they married on June 22, 1894, and had their honeymoon in Coney Island. ("Cheap," Bess once said, "but glorious.")

Bess's mother, a strict German Catholic woman, was very upset that her daughter had married a Jewish man. So they had a second marriage ceremony to make her happy. They also held a third service with a rabbi. Bess used to say "I'm the most married woman I know. . . . I've been married three times and all to the same man."

Up to this point, Houdini's mother had been the most important woman in Houdini's life. Bess even recognized that "Houdini's love for his mother had dominated his life completely." But Mrs. Weiss welcomed Bess into the family.

Throughout his life, Harry Houdini was very affectionate toward Bess. He always wrote her sentimental love letters, sometimes even from the next room in the same house. They never had any children. Instead, they often kept dogs as pets. A dog named Charlie traveled with them everywhere.

Their marriage was a partnership. Harry trusted Bess with all his secrets. She was not only Harry Houdini's wife, but also the new partner in his act.

CHAPTER THREE

A TRAVELING ENTERTAINER

The Houdinis started their career where the Brothers Houdini left off—in dime museums. Houdini tirelessly promoted their act with flyers and pamphlets, urging people to come and see "Mysterious Harry and La Petite Bessie." Bessie did a song-and-dance act, and Houdini performed some simple tricks and escaped from handcuffs. Then, together, they astounded audiences with the Metamorphosis trunk trick.

The equipment for Metamorphosis was a trunk and a cabinet that closed with a curtain. In a magazine article of the time, a reporter described the illusion: "Houdini's next request was that his committee securely encase him in the previously examined sack, tightly bind its mouth together with heavy tape already in their hands, and secure the knots with sealing wax." Sealed up in this way, Houdini was placed inside the trunk.

Assistants locked the trunk, tied it with ropes, and placed it in the cabinet. Houdini shouted from inside the trunk to prove he was still there. Then, Bess clapped her hands three times, closed the curtain, and left. At the same time, the curtain was opened—by Houdini himself! Then, Houdini reopened the trunk and Bess emerged from inside it. What amazed audiences about this trick was that within seconds, Houdini seemed to be replaced by Bess.

One of Houdini's advertising cards from 1895 reads that the Metamorphosis trick had "created a sensation in Europe, Australia, and America." Harry and Bess had never performed outside of America, but exaggerating the popularity of the trick helped draw audiences.

DIME MUSEUMS

The life of traveling entertainers was not easy. Harry and Bess moved from city to city, staying at one rooming house after another. They often played at Kohl and Middleton, a dime museum in Chicago. When they couldn't find work anywhere else, they could almost always find a job there. But even when they had a job, their schedule was tiring. They performed ten to twenty shows a day, working from ten in the morning until ten at night.

Their act was performed on the "curio stage,"

Houdini knew how to get publicity. He used this poster to promote Mysterious Harry and La Petite Bessie's Metamorphosis tour.

which is where the "freaks" were displayed. *Freaks* was the term used at that time to describe people who were physically deformed or so large, thin, small, or tall that they entertained a gawking crowd with their appearance. Even though it seems cruel today, freaks were a popular attraction at the time. Harry and Bess's job was to entertain the people before the freaks performed. Houdini had fond memories of the people he befriended, including Unthan the legless wonder, the large lady Big Alice, and Blue Eagle, "who broke boards over his head to show the solidity of his cranium."

Even though it was an exhausting and odd life for a newly married couple, Houdini used his time in dime museums to develop his skills. "When I was playing dime museums, and being classed a 'freak,' " he said, "I generally kept very quiet and tried to make a living, not knowing I was developing my dexterity by working ten to fifteen times daily."

While playing at a dime museum known as Huber's Palace Museum in New York in 1895, Harry and Bess thought they had received a big break. Tony Pastor's Theater in New York, the leading vaudeville house at the time, had booked them to perform. Vaudeville shows consisted of many different acts, such as dancing, singing, or magic. Vaudeville houses, where many of the top entertainers performed, offered the best jobs. But when they got to Tony Pastor's, their names on the promotional flyer were barely readable. The theater had scheduled them to play during the least busy show times. No one noticed them.

MAKING ENDS MEET

Harry and Bess needed to find a way to make more money. Ever since nine-year-old Houdini performed as Ehrich, Prince of the Air, Houdini had loved the circus. So, later in 1895, Harry and Bess joined the Welsh Brothers' Circus, a small traveling group that toured eastern towns.

Bess sang, danced, and did a mind-reading routine. Harry did magic tricks and his handcuff

Harry and Bess (seated at the right end of the first row) worked hard in the Welsh Brothers' Circus.

act. And they participated in the parade. For this, they were paid "twenty-five a week and cakes [or meals]." Houdini also had to play the role of Projea the Wild Man, who was supposed to be from the jungle and "lived on a diet of raw meat, cigarettes, and cigars." The Wild Man was such a hit that he became a permanent feature in the circus.

At the end of the circus season, even after sending half of their income home to Mrs. Weiss, Harry and Bess had saved some money. In 1896, they invested it in a show touring Canada. But when the show started losing money, they pulled out and went back to the traveling life, picking up engagements wherever and whenever they could. Once, they got off the train in St. Louis, Missouri, without any money. The train station held their trunk and all the equipment for their act. They needed twenty dollars to get their belongings back. But how could they make the money to pay the fee without their equipment?

Harry and Bess had learned a lot on the road and knew how to think fast. They made up a new act called "The Rahners—Harry and Bess—America's Greatest Comedy Act," and a music hall booked them for a one-week engagement paying thirty dollars. The show, which consisted of jokes they had collected from comic magazines, was such a success that the theater manager let them stay on for another week. When they had enough money to get back their props, and the manager found out they had a magic act too, he let them stay a third week.

MIND READERS

In 1897, money was tight, and the Houdinis couldn't find work at any vaudeville theaters or dime museums. They had to settle for the least-respected performance venue—the traveling medicine show. In this kind of show, a group of entertainers traveled from town to town giving performances and selling homemade medicines. The Houdinis joined Dr. Hill's California Concert Company for twenty-five dollars a week.

Harry, Bess, and the rest of the troupe would arrive in a small town in the Midwest, set up on a street corner, and entertain the townspeople with music and singing. Houdini played the tambourine, and Bess sang. After a crowd had gathered, Dr. Hill would sell his homemade medicine and announce a show that evening in a local hall. At these evening performances, Houdini had a chance to show off his magic.

The show wasn't as successful as Dr. Hill had hoped, and he suggested that Harry and Bess spice up their act by pretending to be spirit mediums. Spiritualism—the study of the spirit world—was a popular trend at that time, and mediums were people who could supposedly contact the dead, read minds, and predict the future. In order to fool their audiences into believing they could contact the dead, Harry and Bess would visit cemeteries when they entered a town and memorize the names. They also listened to local gossip and paid people to tell them secrets. Then they would wow the crowd with facts about those who had died.

Harry and Bess also created a special mind-reading routine that stumped their audiences. For example, Bess might have an audience member write down a number, and Harry would try to guess that number. If the person wrote the number 546,782, Bess would say: "Tell now, mind reader. Please speak quickly and answer!" and Harry would recite the number easily.

It seemed impossible, but it was actually very simple. Harry and Bess had developed a code. Each word they said represented a number: Pray=1, Answer=2, Say=3, Now=4, Tell=5, Please=6, Speak=7, Quickly=8, Look=9, and Be quick=10.

All they had to do was memorize the code, and Harry could guess any number after Bess spoke her undetectable message. They used a similar code to represent letters of the alphabet.

Even with the spirit medium routine, the medicine show flopped in 1898. For a while, Harry and Bess performed as mediums on their own and twice they made guesses about other people that turned out to be true. Playing with others' emotions in this way made them uncomfortable. So they stopped being spirit mediums.

In 1898, they spent another season with the Welsh Brothers' Circus, and Houdini even thought of becoming a professional acrobat. But he decided to devote more time to his real love—escapes.

CHALLENGING THE POLICE

As Houdini had discovered in his dime museum and circus acts, audiences weren't really interested in watching him escape from handcuffs. They always thought Houdini's cuffs had been fixed to open easily. Houdini tried to come up with ways to make his escapes more interesting for the spectators.

A few years earlier, Houdini had thought of visiting police stations. He would challenge them to lock him up in their own handcuffs, and then he would escape from them. One of his earliest attempts took place at a police station in Holyoke, Massachusetts. The warden handcuffed Houdini's wrists and closed him up in a room. In less than a minute, Houdini was out of the room with the cuffs undone. The next day, the local paper told the story of his escape, impressed that Houdini unlocked the handcuffs with "as much ease as if they were strings wound around his wrist."

Newspaper stories were a perfect way for Houdini to get free press for his act, so he challenged and escaped from police stations in many other towns. But even though the newspapers always reported his marvelous feats, the towns were small, and the big theaters never noticed.

At the end of 1898, Houdini decided that the only way to get enough attention was to challenge a police station in a big city. He made friends with some local news reporters in Chicago, who introduced him to Andy Rohan, a lieutenant of detectives in the Chicago police department. Harry and Bess visited Rohan in the city jail, and while Bess kept Rohan occupied, Houdini studied the jail's lock system.

Houdini then issued the challenge—he could be handcuffed and locked in a cell, and he would be able to escape. Rohan accepted because he wanted to teach Houdini a lesson. Rohan wanted to prove that no one could escape from Chicago's jail.

With Rohan and all the reporters present, Houdini was handcuffed and locked in a cell. Everyone went to the warden's office to wait. But only a minute later, Houdini walked in, free from the cell and handcuffs unlocked.

The reporters were not impressed though.

After all, Houdini had visited the jail just a few days before and could have made his own set of keys. So Houdini offered to do it again, this time stripped of all his clothes and searched for keys. The police agreed and even sealed Houdini's lips with plaster in case he was hiding a key in his mouth. Again, they bound him in handcuffs, locked him in a cell, and left to see how long it would take him to get out—if he could escape at all. Within ten minutes, Houdini was back in the warden's office, handcuffs in hand—and fully dressed!

The next day, the story appeared in Chicago's newspapers with a picture. Houdini had done the impossible. He was so excited by the article that he bought copies to mail to all the theaters. A few days later, Hopkins Theater, Chicago's top vaudeville house, paid him a visit. They needed someone to fill the star spot (the performance just before the finale). Houdini asked for star billing, $1,000 a week, and a private dressing room with a large mirror. The engagement was for only a few weeks and they needed someone in a hurry, so they agreed.

Harry and Bess had to return to dime museums after their engagement at Hopkins Theater and by the end of 1898 they were broke again. Finances were so bad that Houdini wrote, "I contemplated quitting the show business, and retiring to private life . . . and opening a school of magic."

Houdini even sent out a catalog and called his enterprise Professor Harry Houdini's School of Magic. In the catalog, he advertised booklets on magic and props for tricks. He even offered to sell two of his most popular tricks: a needle-swallowing stunt and the Metamorphosis trick. Lucky for Houdini, no one bought them. For the rest of his career, they were among his most spectacular tricks.

CHAPTER FOUR

LAUNCHING INTO STARDOM

Early 1899 brought a turning point in Houdini's career that launched him into stardom. In St. Paul, Minnesota, at a beer hall called the Palmgarden, a group of theater managers came in to see Houdini's show. Martin Beck, owner of the Orpheum circuit, the largest group of vaudeville theaters in the West, was among them. He challenged Houdini on stage to escape from the handcuffs he had brought with him. Of course, Houdini escaped.

Beck was so impressed that after the show, he sent Houdini a telegram that said, "You can open Omaha March twenty sixth, sixty dollars, will see act probably make you proposition for all next season." Across the bottom of the telegram, Houdini later wrote, "This wire changed my whole Life's journey."

Not only were Harry and Bess earning more

on the Orpheum circuit than they had ever earned before, but the schedule was less hectic. Shows played twice a day at most, and because vaudeville was so popular, the Orpheum theaters were attractive and clean. Acts often spent a week or more in each city.

Houdini traveled all over the large cities of the West and also played eastern theaters because of the Orpheum's connections there. His salary grew along with his popularity. He was hired at $60 a week, and after a year under Beck, Harry made $400 a week—almost as much as a factory worker made in a year.

His act consisted of Metamorphosis and the introduction of the so-called Hindoo Needle Trick, "taught to me by Hindoos at the World's Fair in 1893. The trick is to have a committee inspect hands and mouth; you then swallow forty to fifty sewing needles, then a bunch of thread, and bring them up all threaded."

On April 10, 1899, at the Kansas City Orpheum, a reporter described the famous trick. A committee watched Houdini place the sewing needles in his mouth. Loudly, he chewed them up. "You can hear the steel crunch and snap under his iron teeth," the reporter said. Houdini opened his mouth, and the committee checked that the needles were gone. Then, Houdini began to swallow a long piece of white thread, which the committee

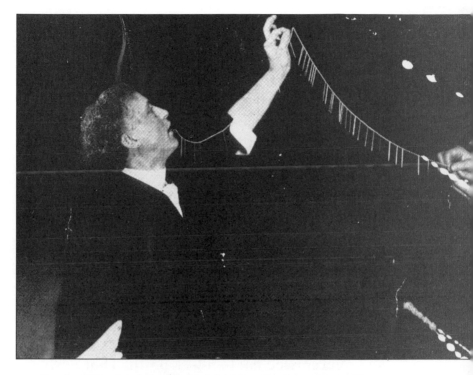

*In the Hindoo Needle Trick, Houdini swallowed
needles and thread and then pulled them from
his mouth—threaded!*

knotted in a special way to help identify it later.
The reporter went on: "This operation is continued
until only the smallest particle of an end is visible
in his throat. Then with open mouth and in the
glare of a bright light, he catches the end of the
thread and slowly draws forth, not only the same
knotted thread, but on this thread are strung the

identical number and kind of needles given him by his judges."

THE KING OF HANDCUFFS

Houdini worked hardest on his handcuff escapes during his tour on the Orpheum circuit. He continued to increase the danger of this act. While he made escaping look easy, the danger was real. Often the cuffs left his arms and legs bloody, bruised, and swollen.

Houdini told the *Washington Post* how he first became interested in handcuffs. Like many of Houdini's stories, it is hard to know what is true about his youth, and what he made up for promotion. "I started in the show business when I was a youngster," he said, "but my mother took me out and apprenticed me to a locksmith. That is where I got my first knowledge of the weakness of locks. I discovered a method of opening them which I kept to myself."

Critics claimed that Houdini's ability to open locks wasn't such a big secret. They said that all handcuffs made by a given manufacturer could be opened by one key, and there weren't that many types made. They believed Houdini owned a few keys that opened all kinds of locks.

Houdini was furious. It was true, and no secret, that all handcuffs of the same model by the

Houdini as the King of Handcuffs

same manufacturer could be opened by the same key. But there were hundreds of kinds of handcuffs being used all over the world. How could Houdini possibly have keys to them all?

Houdini wanted to prove himself to his fans. He issued another challenge to the prison at the San Francisco police department. He would perform an escape completely naked—so there was no way to hide a key.

On July 13, 1899, he arrived at the station. A police surgeon examined Houdini's entire body from his hair to his toes. The detectives locked ten pairs of cuffs on his wrists and ankles, and another pair fastened the wrist and ankle cuffs together. They even taped his mouth shut and placed him in a closet. Miraculously, five minutes later, he emerged with the cuffs strung together.

How was Houdini able to escape after he had been searched so thoroughly? Some people thought he was able to dislocate his bones and therefore make his wrists smaller so that he could slip out easily. Others believed he had magical powers. Houdini's real secret was simple. He had a collection of keys and metal wires to pick the locks.

In the case of the San Francisco police department escape, it is hard to know where he might have hidden his key. It is known that during escapes where he was stripped naked, he would often hide picks in unlikely places, such as his thick, wiry hair. Or it is possible that he hid the pick in the thick skin in the sole of his foot.

Throughout his career, Houdini shipped trunks holding his props from place to place. Trunk No. 8 held his greatest secrets. (Only he, Bess, and his closest assistants knew what was inside.) Years after Houdini died, a magic collector found Trunk No. 8 and described its contents. There were lots of tools—everything from sewing needles to axes, saws, chisels, files, wrenches, and a blowtorch. Among the tools was a box labeled "Handcuff and Leg Iron Keys." It held a collection of about forty-five keys, some of which Houdini designed himself. His skill during an escape lay in the fact that he could instantly identify the key he needed. He also trained his right and left hand to work equally well. "The method adopted by me to acquire this end was, when at table I practiced [using] the left hand persistently, until I could use it almost as easily as the right." He also trained his toes to work like fingers.

After the San Francisco escape and during his tour with the Orpheum, Houdini's success soared. He was called "one of the biggest hits in the history of the Orpheum," and he advertised his handcuff act as "one of the greatest magical feats since biblical times." His growing ego fed his popularity even more. In an effort to appear exotic and foreign, he often claimed to have just arrived from Hungary.

When the tour with the Orpheum ended, Houdini and Bess went out on their own, but they didn't get the publicity they were used to. They neared poverty again. The century was about to change, and Houdini and Bess decided that they were ready for a change too. Since they were able to take America by storm, why not try Europe? Houdini had a new name for himself—Harry Houdini, the King of Handcuffs. They weren't booked for any engagements overseas, but they decided to take the chance. On May 30, 1900, they set sail for England.

THE ALHAMBRA

After a long ocean journey, during which Houdini suffered from seasickness, the two arrived in London. Right away, Houdini started publicizing. His flyers announced, "Who created the biggest Sensation in California since the Discovery of Gold in 1849? WHY! HARRY HOUDINI! The ONLY recognized and Undisputed King of Handcuffs and Monarch of Leg Shackles."

Many American magicians had done well in London, and Houdini was hoping for some attention. They met Harry Day, an agent's assistant, who persuaded the Alhambra Theatre to give

Harry an audition. On June 27, 1900, Houdini auditioned before the London press and detectives from Scotland Yard, London's police headquarters, who brought cuffs for Houdini to escape from. Everyone loved him. The next day the press called him "a marvelous gentleman, who frees himself in marvelously quick fashion of fetters, manacles, and all sorts of frightful things." The Alhambra booked Houdini for two weeks at £60 (about $100 today) per week.

Before Houdini's first show, an escape artist popular in Europe named Cirnoc tried to destroy Houdini's act. He called Houdini a fraud. But when Cirnoc couldn't escape from the same cuffs, Cirnoc actually helped Houdini more than harmed him. "He tried to ruin my show," Houdini said, "but only succeeded in making my opening night a sensation."

Houdini's acts drew large audiences at the Alhambra. Every night, challengers brought him handcuffs, and every night Houdini escaped from them. Houdini was so popular that the Alhambra continued his act until the end of August.

The Alhambra was the most elegant theater Houdini and Bess had ever worked in, and Houdini was treated well. The Alhambra billed him as King of Handcuffs and the World's Greatest Mystifier. Back in the United States, Martin Beck was hoping that Houdini would return. But Houdini had many offers in Europe and planned to stay for a while.

TOURING EUROPE

Over the next five years, Houdini and Bess traveled from country to country—England, Germany, France, and Russia. In Germany, Houdini faced some anti-Semitism. He had always felt free of it in the United States: "It may exist in America, but never that I have known. I never was ashamed to acknowledge that I was a Jew, and never will be, but it is awful what I hear from people that are Jew Haters." In 1901, one German cop claimed Houdini was a fraud. He said it was impossible for anyone, much less an American Jew, to escape Germany's strongest cuffs. Houdini sued him. In court after court, he proved his ability to escape to judge and jury until he won his case.

"[Anti-Semitism] may exist in America, but never that I have known. I never was ashamed to acknowledge that I was a Jew, and never will be, but it is awful what I hear from people that are Jew Haters."

Everywhere Houdini went in Europe, he charmed his audience. Houdini wrote, "Most of my success in Europe was due to the fact that I lost no time in stirring up local interest in every town I played." Tickets sold out days before his performances. All the best theaters in Europe wanted Houdini's act. But along with success came rivals. Many people tried to prove Houdini was a fraud.

On October 24, 1902, during a show in Blackburn, England, a man named William Hope Hodgson presented Houdini with six pairs of heavy iron handcuffs. Houdini inspected them and found that Hodgson had tampered with them. Although Houdini had always vowed never to use cuffs that had been rigged not to open, he did not want to fail the cheering audience. So he allowed Hodgson to lock him in the cuffs.

Behind a cabinet, Houdini was taking longer to escape than audiences were used to. After fifteen minutes, the cabinet was lifted, and Houdini was lying on his side, still bound. He needed to be lifted up. Then the cabinet was replaced. After twenty minutes more, he called for the cabinet to be lifted again. He said that his arms were numb and asked to have the cuffs unlocked for a moment to restore his circulation. But Hodgson wouldn't let him unlock the cuffs. (He was afraid Houdini wanted to see how they worked.)

After another fifteen minutes, Houdini yelled out that one hand was free. Then, finally, after about two hours, Houdini emerged from behind the cabinet with his clothes torn and his arms bleeding. The audience went wild with excitement.

Houdini often tortured himself in this way for his audiences. He wanted them to think he could overcome any challenge. He often emerged bloody and bruised, or was ill for days afterward. Some critics still claimed he would take longer than needed, even reading a newspaper behind the cabinet to waste time while building up the suspense and drama. Regardless of how he did it, Houdini was a true showman.

Houdini controlled the audience the way the best performers do. He knew how to keep people's attention.

Suppose I want to use a short flight of steps from the stage down to the audience. I never have a carpet on them, because while I am transferring a watch or producing an egg from a hat I tramp heavily, and so draw your attention to my feet. If I think the audience is watching me too closely, I signal my assistant to drop something, or to make some sudden movement. If I want a chair, table, or basket brought on the stage, and don't want you to see it, I simply walk to the opposite side of the stage.

Another famous trick during his time in Europe was the coffin trick. "Houdini, the Handcuff King and Prison Breaker, was announced to have accepted a most unique challenge which he would try in front of the spectators," the *Glasgow Herald* reported on September 22, 1904. Houdini climbed into a wooden coffin that was nailed and roped shut. The cabinet was lowered over it and "For an interval of about fifteen minutes the spectators, consumed with curiosity, waited for something." Then Houdini emerged. "Covered with smiles and sweat, the mystifier was minus his hats and boots, while his clothes and collar were crumpled. Houdini had all evidence of a stern struggle . . . but the box was left as if untouched. Not a nail was loosed, nor was one of the three binding ropes tampered with. It was all very mystifying."

Within the week, an imitator performed Houdini's trick to show how easy it was. But Houdini used his critics to get more publicity. His motto was "Do others or they will do you." Houdini redid his trick, first explaining how his critic performed it—he had simply used a certain type of screw that made it easy to push out the ends of the coffin.

Then Houdini did the trick again. The screws were tightened, and the lid closed. Houdini invited a committee to add more screws of their own.

Some people marked their screws to be sure they didn't move. Some stuck stamps over them, so they could tell if they had been tampered with. The cabinet was lowered, and Houdini appeared within minutes.

Obviously, Houdini had a secret of his own. Instead of pushing out the ends of the coffin, Houdini had been able to escape out the bottom. Because of the way he had built the sides attached to the bottom, he simply had to push the coffin up (with its top still on), escape easily, and put the coffin back in place on its base. But the audience was thrilled. Even when his critics seemed to reveal his secrets, Houdini was still full of surprises.

IMITATORS

Houdini wanted to be the best escape artist of his time and did not want other magicians imitating his tricks. But many people tried. "In England we have fifty-five Kings of Handcuffs," he said. "If you throw a stone in the air it will fall down and hit someone who has a handcuff key in his pocket and a 'Handcuff King' idea in his head." According to Houdini, many imitators even imitated his name: "Hourdene, Whodini, Cutini, Stillini, etc."

Houdini decided to create an imitator of his own—his younger brother, Dash. Dash met up with Harry and Bess in Germany. Houdini had

Houdini sent his brother Dash on tour in Europe as
a Houdini imitator called Hardeen.

arranged an act for him that was a copy of Houdini's act, including a trunk, handcuffs, and straitjacket. He and Dash came up with the name Hardeen—it echoed "Houdini," but was still unique. Hardeen was a hit, but always recognized as a Houdini copy. The magic magazine *Mahatma* noted, "Hardeen has made a wonderful reputation in Europe. [He has] made quite a sensation coming right after his brother, and is acknowledged as the best copy of Houdini in the profession today." Now, Houdini even had control of the competition. By 1905, he was the highest-paid vaudeville entertainer in Europe.

CHAPTER FIVE

GROWING DANGERS AND NEW CHALLENGES

Houdini was thoroughly enjoying his time in Europe, but he greatly missed his family back in the United States, especially his mother. He had returned a few times since he had been in Europe, once to buy a twenty-six room mansion on 278 West 113th Street in New York City for Bess, his mother, and himself. Its lavish bathroom included a large mirror in front of which Houdini practiced his escapes. The basement workshop was perfect for building equipment. Houdini also moved in his theater memorabilia that he had collected in Europe.

When Houdini returned to the United States in the summer of 1905, however, it would be for a while. He signed on with the Orpheum circuit for three more years. Although he traveled all over the country, he was not enjoying the same fame he

Houdini with his mother, Cecilia, and wife, Bess

had in Europe. He had to regain his reputation in America.

Jail escapes were still a good way to build his fame in the United States. One of Houdini's most famous took place in 1906 in Washington, D.C. The warden challenged Houdini to try to escape the new locks he had installed on Murderers' Row—the block of cells that held prisoners awaiting death by execution. It was the same prison that held Charles Guiteau, the assassin of President James A. Garfield about twenty-five years earlier. Houdini thought it would be great publicity to escape from Guiteau's former cell.

Houdini was stripped naked and locked behind the bars. The prisoners on Murderers' Row watched as Houdini pulled pieces of wire from his hair, from between his toes, and from under the prison bars. Within minutes, he escaped from the cell. But he was not finished yet. He also unlocked the doors of the prisoners' cells and locked the prisoners in different cells. Then he dressed and went out to meet the officials.

In addition to jail escapes, Houdini escaped from safes, piano boxes, mail pouches, and straitjackets. He saw his first straitjacket in an insane asylum in 1908. "Previous to this incident I had seen and used various restraints such as insane restraint muffs, belts, bedstraps, etc., but this was the first time I saw a straitjacket and it left so vivid an impression on my mind that I hardly slept that night, and in such moments as I slept I saw nothing but straitjackets, maniacs, and padded cells!" Houdini started using a straitjacket in his act, at first escaping from behind a curtain. But people thought he was fak-

> **"This was the first time I saw a straitjacket and it left so vivid an impression on my mind that I hardly slept that night."**

ing, so he did it in full view of the audience, tossing and writhing on the floor in front of the spectators to show off his athletic skill.

NEW ADDITIONS

Houdini wanted to try something new—something more dangerous to draw his audience. An avid swimmer in his youth, Houdini found ways to use water in his escapes. His new home in New York had an oversized bathtub where he practiced holding his breath for as long as three minutes. He would also fill the tub with ice water to see if he could stand the cold temperatures. Putting his body through these tests prepared him for new additions to his act. Handcuffs were still important, but now they were merely accessories to even greater stunts.

The milk can trick, one of Houdini's most adventurous stunts, was first performed on January 5, 1908. On stage stood an iron milk can, large enough to hold one person. All its seams were riveted and soldered so that they were watertight.

While assistants filled the can with twenty-two pails of water, Houdini walked off stage and changed into a bathing suit. His assistants handcuffed him, and he climbed into the can. He challenged the audience to hold their breath along with him, to see how long they could last. He ducked underwater, the lid was screwed and pad-

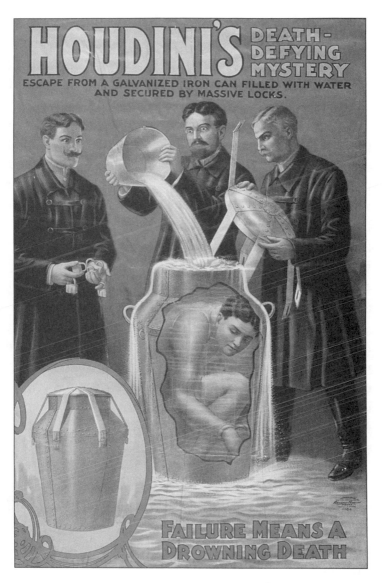

*This dramatic poster advertises Houdini's
daring milk can escape.*

locked shut, and the curtains were drawn. After three minutes—and long after the audience had lost its breath—Houdini emerged from behind the curtain, sopping wet but free. And the can sat in the same spot, with all its locks still in place!

How did he do it? Like all his tricks, this one too was an illusion. The rivets were actually fakes. Only two held the top on. Once inside, Houdini had to unscrew just the two rivets. Then he stood up, lifted off the top, and replaced it. He never had to tamper with the locks. There were even air holes in the lid in case something went wrong. The milk can trick appeared to be too dangerous for anyone else to try, so Houdini didn't have to worry about imitators.

Another popular stunt of Houdini's was jumping, fully shackled, from bridges into rivers and resurfacing unshackled. Off the familiar surroundings of a stage, this stunt was much more impressive. He jumped from bridges all over America, and the newspapers often reported his stunts on their front pages. In 1906, he was booked at the Temple Theater in Detroit for two weeks and wanted to advertise his act. What better way to get attention than a public outdoor event? Tied up in two sets of handcuffs, Houdini jumped from the Bell Isle Bridge into the cold Detroit River on November 27, 1906.

Details of the story have been exaggerated over the years. One version says that the river was actually frozen, and a hole had to be cut into the ice for Houdini. When he tried to surface, the current had pulled him far from the hole. An assistant had to throw a rope down, and finally, Houdini, who had been breathing the air between the water and the ice, pulled himself out.

According to weather records, November 27 was a cold day but not cold enough to freeze the river. However, according to the *Detroit News*, he did make a jump. On the front page the story read:

Tied by a lifeline 113 feet [35 m] long, handcuffed with two of the best and latest model handcuffs, [Houdini] leaped from the drawn

Around the country, Houdini's jumps from bridges in handcuffs and padlocks drew large crowds.

span of the Belle Isle Bridge at 1 o'clock this afternoon, freed himself from the handcuffs while under water, then swam to a waiting lifeboat, [where he] passed over the unlocked and open cuffs and clambered aboard.

After that successful jump, the theater was packed for the rest of his engagement. Houdini had regained his popularity in America.

THE UNMASKING

Houdini had other interests besides illusions and stunts. He always liked writing. One of his pursuits was *Conjurers' Monthly Magazine*, a journal he started in 1906. Houdini used it as a platform to expose his imitators and advertise his opinions about the trade.

In *Conjurers' Monthly*, Houdini published an essay called "Unknown Facts Concerning Robert-Houdin." Although Robert-Houdin had been Houdini's namesake and role model, Houdini now changed his opinion. Some believe it was because of his bitterness toward Robert-Houdin's daughter-in-law, who never gave Houdini permission to visit Robert-Houdin's grave. Or perhaps Houdini felt it necessary to triumph over any magician—past or present.

Whatever the reason, Houdini began to research Robert-Houdin's tricks—tricks that Robert-Houdin had claimed to have devised himself. Houdini was able to trace the invention of these tricks to earlier magicians. So in 1908, Houdini expanded his article in *Conjurers' Monthly* into a book, *The Unmasking of Robert-Houdin*.

True to character, Houdini was a hardworking writer. In his diary, he noted, "Wrote until 2:30 A.M. on Houdin book. This is a labor of love. I shall be happy when it is finished as it will take a lot of worry off my mind."

TO THE SKIES

Houdini had another hobby. In 1908, Houdini became obsessed with flying. Powered flight was a relatively new invention—the Wright brothers had performed their first flight only five years earlier.

In 1909, Houdini purchased the latest in aviation technology—a Voisin plane. Now he needed someone to teach him how to fly it. But flying was so new that there were only about twenty aviators in the world, and certainly no flying schools. But Houdini was able to find a Frenchman, named Brassac, to teach him how to fly.

In early 1910, he was scheduled for a show in Australia and insisted on taking his plane with him. No one had yet flown on the Australian continent, and Houdini wanted to be the first. On March 16, 1910, Houdini flew 1 mile (1.6 km) at Digger's Rest near Melbourne, winning the prize as the first person to fly in Australia. He had found something to conquer, and he had won. But flying was a short-lived hobby. Right after he won the

Houdini sits in the cockpit of his Voisin biplane in Australia.

Australian Prize, it was time to focus on magic again. He left Australia, never to fly again.

UNDERWATER

Between 1910 and 1913, Houdini performed shows in Europe and the United States. He added a few new exciting stunts to his act, always getting more complex and dangerous. Again, both of his new stunts involved water.

Houdini referred to his Chinese water torture cell trick as "the old Upside-Down" or "U.S.D." Some have called it his greatest escape. It was introduced in Berlin, Germany, on September 21, 1912. Bound in handcuffs, Houdini had his ankles locked into a block of wood. Then he was lowered headfirst into a glass booth about the size of a small phone booth, filled with water. Assistants locked the steel lid tight. Within minutes, Houdini escaped. (The inside of the tank was actually lined with iron bars that Houdini could climb up with his head and shoulders. At the top, he could release the locks easily and escape.)

For another exciting water escape, Houdini was back outside again. Instead of jumping off bridges, Houdini would be locked inside a heavy iron box and then dropped into the river. He performed the trick in 1912 in New York City. Manacled inside the heavily weighted box, Houdini was

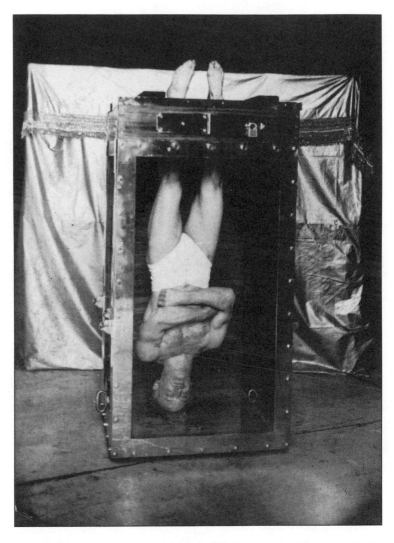

In his Chinese water torture cell trick, a handcuffed Houdini escapes upside down from a glass booth filled with water.

about to be dropped into the Hudson River. But the police swooped in at the last moment to stop it—it was against the law to jump off a New York pier.

Instead, the box—and Houdini—were placed in a tugboat and dropped into the river. After only fifty-seven seconds, Houdini popped up above the surface of the water. He was greeted with deafening cheers.

After this trick, and a very successful week in New York, he asked for his payment in gold coins. Much as he had done as a child begging in the streets in winter, he brought the coins to his mother and dumped them into her lap proudly.

OBSESSION WITH DEATH

Houdini was obsessed with death. Early in his life, he picked out his own tombstone and gravesite. He often visited cemeteries. This obsession became increasingly apparent. From his first milk can escape in 1908, Houdini's tricks grew more dangerous. Houdini wanted his escapes to be truly challenging, not just to appear difficult.

One stunt was not a success. Houdini had decided to escape from being buried alive. He practiced by burying himself in a casket underground and then digging himself out. He was successful when just a few feet of dirt were placed over the casket. But when he attempted the trick under

6 feet (1.8 m) of dirt, the actual depth of a grave, he panicked. Frantically digging, he tried to shout, but his mouth filled with dirt. He knew very well that panicking was the most dangerous thing he could do, but he couldn't help himself. He finally surfaced, but he never attempted this stunt again. He had come too close to real death.

Houdini's tricks were a series of attempts to defeat death—he put himself in very dangerous situations and always survived. But one death he could not control. On July 17, 1913, after a show in Copenhagen, Denmark, Houdini received a telegram from New York. His mother had died of a stroke.

Mrs. Weiss had always been one of the most important people in Houdini's life. He once said, "If God ever permitted an Angel to walk the earth in human form, it was my Mother." For months after her death, Houdini was very depressed and could think of nothing but his beloved mother.

After her death, Houdini's tricks grew even more dangerous, as if he was testing death for himself. He added the suspended straitjacket escape to his collection. It would be the last stunt he would ever invent. He traveled from city to city, hanging upside down from the tallest buildings, wiggling out of a straitjacket in front of thousands of spectators below. The danger was very real, but Houdini defeated death each and every time, as always.

Houdini's suspended straitjacket escape was his last new stunt.

HOUDINI THE FILMMAKER

By 1916, Houdini was ready for a change. The stress of stunt life was tiring now that he was forty-two years old. He was still a world-class performer, but vaudeville was not as popular as it had been. Houdini decided on a new career in film. The first American motion-picture theater opened in Pennsylvania in 1905, and by 1915, thousands of theaters had opened across America and motion pictures were becoming as popular as vaudeville.

By 1923, Houdini had made five major silent movies. He founded Houdini Pictures Corporation, a production company where he played various roles—actor, writer, director, producer, and stuntman. Unfortunately, the films were not financial or critical successes.

The films, including *The Master Mystery*, *The Grim Game*, *Terror Island*, and *The Man from Beyond*, were just loose storylines to show off his escapes. In *The Man from Beyond* (a name people often used to refer to Houdini himself), Houdini played a man who had been frozen in a block of ice for many years. When he is chipped out, he must deal with a foreign, modern world. One of the most famous scenes in this movie takes place on the Niagara River, where the leading lady is canoeing and starts drifting toward the falls. The "man from beyond" rushes in at the last moment and saves her from death.

Harry Houdini in a movie still from The Grim Game

Houdini performed all his own stunts, but audiences were not as impressed with the screen version of Houdini. During his live performances, there was always a threat of real danger. But on film, audiences couldn't tell what was real and what was staged.

HOUDINI THE SCHOLAR

Over the years, Houdini had been adding to his huge library collection. He had so much in this home library that he had to hire a full-time librarian to keep track of it all.

His eager desire to collect information may have been due to his lack of formal education. When visiting foreign cities, he scoured through bookshops or bought entire collections of books and letters from magicians or theaters. After one such trip, Houdini wrote, "We have 'arrived' home safe. Am having an awful time with the books I brought back. Never realized the amount, until I tried to get them into my home. It's a good thing I played my entire tour, and was too busy to look at all the bookshops." He even advertised his desire for more books in the *New York Times*: "As I possess the largest collection (private or public) in the world of material regarding magic, magicians, books, scripts, spiritualistic effects, documents, steel engravings, automata, am still looking for anything that would embellish my collection of interest on the subject of magic or mysteries."

Houdini's collection had grown since the publication of his first two books, *The Right Way to Do Wrong* (1906) and *The Unmasking of Robert-Houdin* (1908). So, he distilled some of the interesting research from his collection into another book called *Miracle Mongers and Their Methods* (1921). In it, he describes the methods used by fire-eaters and poison-eaters. It was less of a manual for magicians than a chance for Houdini to show off the information he had collected in his library.

CHAPTER SIX

DISPROVING SPIRITUALISM

Harry and Bess had dabbled in Spiritualism early in their careers while traveling with Dr. Hill's medicine show. The practice of communicating with a "spirit world," where loved ones were believed to reside after death, swept through Europe and the United States at that time. Mediums were people who channeled the words or actions of spirits at gatherings called séances. Mediums often set up their séances in dark rooms, with their audiences seated around a table. This was the best way, they claimed, to connect with the Great Beyond.

Houdini wanted to believe that Spiritualism was real. He firmly believed "in a Supreme Being and that there is a Hereafter." He thought there could be "no greater blessing . . . than the opportunity, once again, to speak to my sainted Mother who awaits me with open arms."

Houdini soon found, however, that Spiritual-

ism was a farce. He could find physical explana-
tions for all the medium's "powers" and knew that
they were only tricks. Why didn't Houdini wel-
come séances as a type of show? After all, he was
in the business of deceiving audiences with his
magic tricks. But the practice of Spiritualism and
its effect on innocent people horrified Houdini.
Houdini took up his pen and wrote another book.
He attacked Spiritualism head-on in A *Magician
among the Spirits* (1924).

WHY TAKE ON SPIRITUALISM?

Why would Houdini want to prove that Spiritualism
was a farce? After all, he and Bess had pretended
to be mediums before. "At the time I appreciated
the fact that I surprised my clients," Houdini
wrote, but he grew to realize that what he was
doing "bordered on crime." Unlike Houdini's stage
tricks, Spiritualism involved people's emotions.
People often visited mediums because they wanted to communicate with a loved one they missed
dearly. Houdini believed mediums cruelly preyed
on a person's sadness and hope. "I have watched
this great wave of Spiritualism sweep the world in
recent months and realized that it has taken such
a hold on persons . . . especially those suffering
from bereavement, that it has become a menace to
health and sanity," Houdini wrote in his book.

Houdini did not make accusations against

spirit mediums without proof or research. "During my last trip abroad, in 1919," he wrote, "I attended over one hundred séances with the sole purpose of honest investigation; these séances were presided over by well-known mediums in France and England. In addition to attending these séances I spent a great deal of time conferring with persons prominently identified with Spiritualism. In the course of my intense investigations I have met most of the famous mediums of our time." (Houdini often visited these séances in disguise.) He also read everything he could on the subject of Spiritualism, but "nothing I ever read covering the so-called Spiritualistic phenomena has impressed me as being genuine."

To test his belief that mediums were frauds, he made deals with fourteen of his friends. If they died before Houdini, they would try to communicate with him. But he never received word from any of them. After all his research, Houdini concluded "nothing has been revealed to convince me that intercommunication has been

"Nothing has been revealed to convince me that intercommunication has been established between the Spirits of the departed and those still in the flesh."

Houdini wore a disguise to investigate fraudulent mediums.

established between the Spirits of the departed and those still in the flesh."

BEGINNINGS OF SPIRITUALISM

One of the key points of *A Magician among the Spirits* was that Spiritualism's very beginnings were based on fraud. Houdini traced Spiritualism back to 1848 when two young girls, Margaret and Kate Fox, found a way to scare their easily frightened mother. They bumped an apple on the floor after their mother had put them to bed. Their mother was convinced that these rappings were signs from a spirit in another world, and that the girls could communicate with it. Margaret and Kate toured as the Fox Sisters for most of their lives.

In the 1860s, two brothers, Ira and William Davenport, made themselves famous with more elaborate shows of Spiritualism. A group of people would watch assistants tie the two brothers securely into a cabinet. Various items, including musical instruments, were placed in the cabinet with them. The assistants closed the doors and turned down the lights. Suddenly, the group would hear the instruments seemingly float around the room. There was no way, the audience believed, that the Davenport brothers could have gotten out of their cabinet.

Medium Ira Davenport (left) with Harry Houdini

Houdini noted, "These brothers have always been, and still are, pointed to as being indisputable proof on the reality and genuineness of mediumistic phenomena." When Houdini and Ira Davenport later became very close friends, Ira confessed the fraudulence of their act. Houdini said, "He frankly admitted that the work of the Davenport brothers was accomplished by perfectly natural means." Ira described to Houdini the way the rope was tied in the cabinet, which allowed the brothers to easily slip out and then slip back in after they had played the instruments around the room. "Strange how people imagine things in the dark!" Ira said. "Why the musical instruments never left our hands, yet many spectators would have taken an oath that they heard them flying over their heads."

METHODS AND EXPLANATIONS

In his book, Houdini also tells about many famous Spiritualists, what they were best known for, and their secrets. The Italian spiritualist Eusapia Pallandino "has to her credit the successful deception of more philosophic and scientific men than any other known medium," wrote Houdini. During séances, audiences heard rappings on the table around which they were all seated, and the table would then rise above the sitters. The sitters on her right and left would be holding her hands and touching their feet to hers the entire time, so it was believed that there was no way she could be causing the rappings and levitation. But Pallandino was crafty, and through extremely slight movements, "she would bring [the sitters'] hands and legs close enough together that one hand and one foot was doing the work for two, allowing the other hand and foot to do her tricks."

Ann O'Delia Diss Debar was known for the writing pad trick. She would present an empty writing pad, hide it away, and return with it filled with writing.

Slate writing was Dr. Henry Slade's specialty. Much like the writing pad trick, Dr. Slade would present the sitters with a collection of small chalkboards, or slates. Each sitter would write down a question. The medium would take the slate, hold it under the table for a time, and return it to the top of the table, with the answer to the question written on it. The solution to this trick was a little more complex. Someone in the room below would reach up through the floor, collect the slate, answer the question, and return the slate to Dr. Slade.

Then there was spirit photography, in which mediums used double exposure to make a dead person's image appear in a photograph. The use of ectoplasm was the grossest trick—a gooey sub-

*Houdini, Bess, and an assistant show one way
slate-writing substitution works.*

stance would come out of a medium's nose or
mouth and form hideous shapes. Houdini was also
appalled by this method, "Up to the present day
nothing has crossed my path to make me think
that the Great Almighty will allow emanations

from a human body of such horrible, revolting, viscous substances."

HOUDINI AND DOYLE

Scientists sat in on many of these séances to judge whether they were genuine. And the scientists were most often the easiest people to fool. Recent discoveries in electricity, radioactivity, and other physical sciences suggested that there were many natural laws not yet understood. So it was easy for the scientists to believe the possibilities mediums set before them. Houdini felt he was a much better judge. After all, his business was to trick people, and he would be more likely to recognize the mediums' tricks.

"Spiritualism has claimed among its followers numbers of brilliant minds. . . . Such a one is Sir Arthur Conan Doyle," Houdini writes. Doyle, best known today as the author of the Sherlock Holmes mysteries, was obsessed with Spiritualism. Houdini and Doyle had been friends since they met in England in 1919. "It would be difficult to determine just when Sir Arthur and I first discussed Spiritualism, but from that talk to the present we have never agreed upon it. Our viewpoints differ; we do not believe the same thing."

Houdini and Doyle even had an experience together that proved to Houdini that Spiritualism was a farce. When visiting the Doyles in Atlantic City, Doyle invited Houdini to take part in a séance with his wife, Lady Doyle, as the medium. They were going to try to contact Houdini's mother. Houdini later explained:

I was *willing* to believe, even *wanted* to believe. . . . I especially wanted to speak to my Mother, because that day, June 17, 1922, was her birthday. (This was not known to Lady Doyle. If it had been my Dear Mother's spirit communicating a message, she, knowing her birthday was my most holy holiday, surely would have commented on it.)

Lady Doyle was "seized by the spirit," grabbed a pencil and pad and started writing. Houdini read the spirit's message, hoping to feel his mother's presence. But he said, "There wasn't even a semblance of it. The more so do I hesitate to believe and accept the above letter because, although my sainted mother had been in America for almost fifty years, she could not speak, read, nor write English."

Yet Doyle still believed. He treated Spiritualism as a religion. And no matter how often Houdini proved mediums to be frauds, Doyle still

Harry Houdini was never able to convince Sir Arthur Conan Doyle, author of the Sherlock Holmes mysteries, that Spiritualism was fraudulent.

believed they were real. He argued that the only reason mediums sometimes cheated was that they were trying too hard to convince their audiences. He believed the Fox sisters were genuine too, even after they admitted to making everything up.

MARGERY

One of Houdini's biggest rivals was a medium named Margery. She was the most convincing medium of the time. The magazine *Scientific American* announced a prize of $5,000 to the first person to produce real spirit contact during a séance. A committee, which consulted with Houdini, was organized to judge if Margery's séances were genuine.

The committee was drawn to Margery because she was able to make lights flash, bugles call, and clocks stop. After careful observation at her séances, the committee from *Scientific American* was ready to award her the prize. Houdini was furious. He knew nothing of Margery and thought the committee was trying to keep him away from their investigation.

Houdini demanded to attend a séance. He sat at Margery's side so he could try to detect her tricks. During the séance, she rang a bell and threw a megaphone, while her hands and legs were supposedly held at both sides.

Margery convinced the other visitors, but Houdini declared she was "one hundred per cent trickster or fraud." He wrote, "There is no doubt in my mind whatsoever that this lady who has been 'fooling' the scientists for months resorted to some of the slickest methods I have ever known and honestly it has taken my thirty years of experience to detect her in her various moves." He had been able to feel her legs moving under the table using a trick of his own. By tying a rubber bandage around his leg all day, he had made his leg swell so much that it had "a much keener sense of feeling," making it easier to notice Margery's movements. Luckily, Houdini had saved *Scientific American* from awarding the prize to a fraud.

PROVING HIMSELF A FAKE

Many people still believed Houdini was a medium, no matter how vehemently he denied it. "Sir Arthur thinks that I have great mediumistic powers and that some of my feats are done with the aid of spirits. Everything I do is accomplished by material means, humanly possible, no matter how baffling it is." But Houdini could never convince others that he didn't have mediumistic powers, without revealing his secrets.

Houdini even held some séances and explained how he did his tricks immediately after they ended. In one, a spirit comes through the window and walks on the ceiling. Houdini had two trained acrobats balancing hand to hand. "I told everyone present that it was only a trick, but as usual they insisted that I was a medium."

CHAPTER SEVEN

A DEATH HE COULD NOT DEFEAT

Houdini's act now consisted of more than just tricks. By the end of 1925, he had developed a show that lasted more than two hours called HOUDINI. It was an extravaganza of tricks and lectures about the history of Spiritualism and fraudulent mediums. Even though Houdini was now more than fifty years old, he was in good health and still had the energy to travel from city to city on tour. He had never rested once during his career. Even when the strain from too many straitjacket escapes had prompted his doctor to insist on a three-month rest, Houdini refused. Once, he broke his ankle during the water torture cell trick, but he still went on with the show. He seemed invincible.

HIS FINAL ACT

In 1926, Houdini was giving one of his lectures on spirit frauds. After the lecture, a young college student named Samuel J. Smilovitch approached Houdini to show him a sketch he had drawn of him. Houdini was pleased with the boy's talent. He made an appointment to have Smilovitch draw an entire portrait of him later in the week in his dressing room at Montreal's Princess Theater, where he would be doing a show.

On October 22, 1926, Smilovitch arrived at Houdini's dressing room with Whitehead and Price, two fellow students. Smilovitch began sketching Houdini, who was lying on a couch reading some mail. Whitehead questioned Houdini about his body strength. Price told the following story of what happened next:

[Whitehead] asked Houdini whether it was true that punches in the stomach did not hurt him. Houdini remarked rather unenthusiastically that his stomach could resist much. . . . Thereupon [Whitehead] gave Houdini some very hammer-like blows below the belt, first securing Houdini's permission to strike him.

While it was probably true that Houdini's strong body could withstand blows to the stomach, Houdini had not had time to prepare himself.

At first, Houdini seemed OK after the punches. But by the end of the day, he had stomach pain.

In true Houdini style, however, he went on with his show at the Princess Theater.

Next stop was Detroit, where he had a show opening on October 24. He and Bess boarded the train from Montreal to Detroit. By this time, Houdini was in so much pain that he couldn't hide it from Bess. Bess telegraphed ahead—she wanted a doctor waiting for them at the hotel to examine Houdini.

But the train was late, and Houdini and Bess went straight to the theater. The doctor examined Houdini in the dressing room. Bess didn't hear the doctor say he thought Houdini had an inflamed appendix and should be taken to the hospital right away. "I'll do this show if it's my last," Houdini responded. The theater was sold out, and he didn't want to let the audience down.

"I'll do this show if it's my last."

But the show did not go on as planned. During the performance, Houdini almost collapsed. The audience noticed that he seemed to be hurrying the show along. Finally, Houdini turned to his assistant and said, "Drop the curtain, Collins, I can't go any further."

Houdini was rushed to Grace Hospital. Doctors there removed his badly burst appendix, which they believed had ruptured on the train to

Detroit. The doctors didn't believe that White-head's punches to Houdini's stomach caused the appendicitis. They believed that Houdini already had appendicitis and that the blows just aggravated the condition.

His family rushed to his bedside, and Houdini held on for a few more days. But then he told his brother, "Dash, I'm getting tired and I can't fight any more." He died on October 31, 1926, at the age of fifty-two.

Houdini's body was taken to New York in the bronze coffin he used for his buried-alive stunt. Long before his death, Houdini had chosen his burial plot and planned his funeral. The funeral was held on November 4, 1926, in New York. About 2,000 people, including members of the Society of American Magicians—which Houdini had been president of from 1912 to 1926—crowded the ballroom and street where the funeral was held.

A MASTER MAGICIAN

Long after his death in 1926, Houdini is still remembered as the master of magicians. All magicians today, from amateur backyard entertainers to superstars hosting television extravaganzas, carry on the showmanship tradition of Harry Houdini.

With his humble beginnings with smaller

Harry Houdini's funeral procession in New York City

tricks, such as sleight-of-hand, card, and rope tricks, Houdini was not just a master magician. He was also a master of illusion, beginning with his very first such trick—Metamorphosis. This trick is still often performed today, and its solution is still unknown to many people. Houdini's grand-scale illusions, such as making an elephant disappear on stage, stunned audiences with the seemingly impossible.

He was also a master escape artist. Nothing could hold him—not the tightest handcuffs, the padlocked water chambers, nor the deepest graves. One writer described his acts as "death and resurrection" shows. He placed himself in extreme danger, near death, and he always survived. When people doubted that he was escaping on his own, he moved his act from behind a curtain and performed in full view of the audience, even hanging upside down above busy streets in his straitjacket escapes.

As a magician, Houdini never claimed that magic was the solution to his tricks, illusions, or stunts. While he wanted to believe in a spirit world, his exhaustive study of Spiritualism proved it false. Harry and Bess had an agreement that when he died, she would try to contact him beyond the grave with their own secret code to prove once and for all whether Spiritualism held any truth. She held a séance every year for ten years without success. Houdini, once again, had proved his point.

While there is no doubt that Houdini was mysterious and pursued knowledge of the supernatural, he always claimed that his tricks were based purely on natural means. His own strength and cleverness—traits of which he was very proud—were the secrets to his success.

Master magician Harry Houdini shows how to slip off handcuffs.

CHRONOLOGY

1874	Born Ehrich Weiss on March 24 in Budapest, Hungary
1878	Settles with family in Appleton, Wisconsin
1883	Performs as Ehrich, Prince of the Air
1887	Moves with family to New York City
1888	Gets a job at H. Richter's Sons, tie manufacturer
1891	Changes his name to Houdini after reading the memoirs of Robert-Houdin
1893	The Brothers Houdini perform at the World's Columbian Exposition in Chicago
1894	Marries Bess Rahner on June 22
1895	Joins Welsh Brothers' Circus; issues the first of his police station challenges in Holyoke, Massachusetts

1897	Joins Dr. Hill's California Concert Company medicine show
1898	Returns for one season with Welsh Brothers' Circus; tries to start Professor Harry Houdini's School of Magic
1899	Tours with the Orpheum circuit
1900	Tours Europe
1905	Returns to the United States
1906	Escapes from the cell of the notorious assassin Charles Guiteau in Washington, D.C.; starts *Conjurers' Monthly Magazine*; performs bridge jumps
1908	Writes *The Unmasking of Robert-Houdin*; introduces the milk can escape
1910	Wins prize for being the first person to fly on the Australian continent on March 16
1910–1913	Travels between the United States and Europe on tour
1912–1926	Serves as president of the Society of American Magicians
1916–1923	Pursues a career in film as actor, writer, director, producer, and stuntman
1921	Writes *Miracle Mongers and Their Methods*

| 1924 | Writes a book attacking Spiritualism called *A Magician among the Spirits* |
| 1926 | Dies of appendicitis on October 31 |

A NOTE ON SOURCES

While Dana Meachen Rau researched this book, she found that no matter how elusive and secretive Houdini may have been about the methods of his tricks and stunts, information about him was easy to find. Houdini was a tireless promoter of his act and kept careful records and diaries of his experiences and thoughts throughout his life. When performing overseas, he often mailed postcards home to remind himself of a specific date or event. Two books that drew on this substantial information were vital in researching this book: *The Life and Many Deaths of Harry Houdini* by Ruth Brandon and *Houdini!!! The Career of Ehrich Weiss* by Kenneth Silverman.

Houdini was a writer himself and held the definitive collection of magic and spiritualistic phenomena in his own personal library. He drew on these in writing his own books, including *A*

Magician among the Spirits, which were a key into the opinions and personality of Houdini.

Because Houdini was such a public figure, there are countless photographs and movies of him that Dana Meachen Rau also used while researching this book. *Houdini: The Great Escape*, a video documentary of Houdini's life, was a vital visual resource as well as an opportunity to see Houdini in action.

FOR MORE INFORMATION

BOOKS

Borland, Kathryn Kilby. *Harry Houdini: Young Magician*. New York: Aladdin, 1991.

Brandon, Ruth. *The Life and Many Deaths of Harry Houdini*. New York: Random House, 1993.

Houdini: The Great Escape. New York: Arts and Entertainment Television Network, 1994.

Houdini, Harry. *A Magician among the Spirits*. North Stratford, NH: Ayer Co. Publishers, 1987.

Lalicki, Tom. *Spellbinder: The Life of Harry Houdini*. New York: Holiday House, 2000.

Milbourne, Christopher. *Houdini: A Pictorial Biography*. New York: Random House, 1998.

Sabin, Louis. *The Great Houdini, Daring Escape Artist*. Mahwah, NJ: Troll Associates, 1990.

Silverman, Kenneth. *Houdini!!! The Career of Ehrich Weiss.* New York: Harper Perennial, 1997.

INTERNET RESOURCES

The Houdini Museum
1433 N. Main
Scranton, PA 18508
(717) 342-5555
**http://www.microserve.net/~magicusa/
houdini.html#listone**
This website of the famous Houdini Museum gives information about its tours, shows, and exhibits.

**The American Variety Stage Collection
http://lcweb2.loc.gov/ammem/vshtml/
vshdini.html**
This website provides a large collection of photographs and other memorabilia devoted to the career of Harry Houdini. The materials are drawn from the Rare Books and Special Collections Division and the Prints and Photographs Division of the Library of Congress.

**Society of American Magicians/
Society of Young Magicians
http://www.uelectric.com/sam/**

This website, hosted by the Society of American Magicians (SAM), provides information about membership, newsletters, events, and magic history. It also has information about joining the Society of Young Magicians (SYM) for young people ages seven to seventeen who practice magic as a hobby.

INDEX

Page numbers in *italics* indicate illustrations.

Society of American Magicians, 92
spirit photography, 81
Spiritualism, 33–34, 74–76, 78, 83–84, 86–89, 94
St. Louis, Missouri, 32–33
St. Paul, Minnesota, 39
straitjacket escapes, *10*, 11, 68, *69*
straitjackets, 9, 57

Temple Theater, 60
Tony Pastor's Theater, 30
trapeze act, 19
traveling medicine show, 33–34
Trunk No. 8, 45

The Unmasking of Robert-Houdin (book), 63, 72

vaudeville theater, 30, 33, 37, 39–40, 54, 70
Voisin biplane, 63, *64*

Washington Post interview, 42
water escapes, 58, 65, *66*, 89, 93
Weiss, Cecilia (mother), 13, 22, 26, 32, 55, *56*, 68, 74
Weiss, Ehrich. *See* Houdini, Harry.
Weiss, Samuel (father), 13, *14*, 17, 22
Weiss, Theodore "Dash," 21–22, *23*, 52, 54, 92
Welsh Brothers' Circus, 31, *31*, 35
World's Columbian Exposition (Chicago), 22
writing pad trick, 81

ABOUT THE AUTHOR

Dana Meachen Rau works as a writer, illustrator, and editor and knows only one card trick. She has authored more than forty children's books, both fiction and nonfiction, including *George Lucas: Creator of Star Wars* in the Book Report Biography series for Franklin Watts. She lives with her husband, Chris, and their son, Charlie, in Farmington, Connecticut.